Praise for *4 Magic Steps to: Double Profit*

"It is a true gift to be able to explain complex ideas simply and clearly and in this book Jeremy does just that. I would recommend *4 Magic Steps* to all management teams and would encourage a re-read on an annual basis. Too often the intricacies of any business conceal the prime objective and distract management. This book reminds us exactly what our priorities should be."

Ted Smith, Chairman Tracscare and Keys Care and former CEO of Craegmoor and Embrace.

"Whenever I look at my business performance, it's as if Squawk is now sitting on my shoulder...."

Gary Smith, former CEO SIS and President Bell, Canada.

"Jeremy Rudd delivers the goods in this very accessible and easy to read business book for everyone. Start-ups to Fortune 500 companies will appreciate the easy to remember approach and the ease with which it can be explained to their teams. His 4 Magic Steps are extremely compelling and the math examples show us just how powerful, how magical they are. Everyone running a business or growing a business should read this book. Cash is king, and Rudd shows us why it is powerful and how to grow profit in 4 easy to understand steps. Buy it, you can't afford not to!"

Trevor Hill, Chairman & CEO, FATHOM. Phoenix, Arizona. www.gwfathom.com.

"Speaking of his predecessors, Sir Isaac Newton, the greatest scientist of his era, once remarked, modestly, that if he had seen further than others, it was because he stood on the shoulders of giants. Let Jeremy's clear and incisive thoughts be the shoulders which help you see further than the competition."

A successful entrepreneur.

"Talk about scratching an itch! Jeremy Rudd addresses the very heart of the problem that every business manager and entrepreneur wrestles with: how can I make my business more profitable? Using a beautifully simple story he brings complex business principles into everyday language, enabling the reader to extract tools that they can instantly apply. Every entrepreneur should read this. Every manager should read this. Everyone should read this."

Piers Clark, Founder & Chairman Isle Group. Isle is a technical, specialist consultancy with offices in the UK, Netherlands, USA, Australia, Singapore and Abu Dhabi. www.isleutilities.com.

"Read this book if you are a busy boss, a struggling SME or an aspiring entrepreneur. The 4 Magic Steps formula will help you to cut through the entanglements and diversions which so often detract from a primary focus of business – profitability. Jeremy has brought to bear his many years of experience in developing and turning around businesses in a wide range of sectors to give you a simple, readable and engaging story exposing the magic steps to doubling your profit. Buy one for yourself and one for every person in your business to remind them to stay focused on this vital element of success and sustainability."

Specialist adviser to and former MD of Facility & Utility Management Businesses.

"I was reviewing business books and had just finished one about the destiny of business using complex terminology such as theory of computability, theorem of transaction costs and finally the law of the distributed ledger – phew I thought, I needed a PHD to understand it! Thankfully I then picked up Jeremy's *4 Magic Steps*. it is a breath of fresh air, a simple, readable and enlightening story leading you through 4 Magic Steps to double your profit. Jeremy has managed to write a user guide for startup and established enterprises that will help anyone develop, analyze and adapt their current business plan to be financially viable.

I enjoyed this book and regret that I did not have such sage advice in designing, building and running two businesses and rescuing a third."

Jerry Peterson. Sarasota, Florida, former CIO, COO, CEO & Chairman of UK and US companies.

"Most businesses stay small, some by design, most not. The focus in this book might help you to have the choice."

UK Business advisor.

"这是我读过的最生动有趣的经济学书！和那些枯燥乏味、冗长复杂的专业书籍相比，它不仅浅显易懂，而且书中的原理也和实际生活工作息息相关。书中的每一个要点都被解释得非常透彻，可以立刻应用到我们的日常工作中。这本书让我一个外行也不由自主的希望可以立刻把书中的原理运用到工作中，把利润翻一番！"

Dr Juan Du, Scientist, City of Hope National Medical Center, California, USA.

"This new book is excellent. It certainly makes a refreshing change from reading tedious business books that are often less accessible and much less well explained! It's a fantastic primer for new entrepreneurs and for top management of businesses who have never had a formal business education and so often fall into the usual traps like underpricing, overtrading/working capital shortage, and not keeping a firm lid on overheads. I particularly liked "Sage" being the accountant with his tins instead of ledgers but I constantly suspected Ted of being a crook who was going to run off with all the cash one day and/or set up as a direct competitor!"

James McNaught-Davis, Managing Partner
Wetherby Capital Partners LLP, London, UK.

"Understandably, a young businessperson switches off when listening to an old codger spouting on about business. I really, really hope young business people don't switch off when confronted with Jeremy's insights into business performance. They may just avoid thirty years of misery and worry."

Old codger, retired retailer.

"An enjoyable and thought-provoking read bringing out a clear focus on the key things for profit that all managers need to concentrate on – whether that's for a large or small business."

David Tydeman, CEO OYSTER Group.

---

4 Magic Steps to:
DOUBLE PROFIT

HOW TO MAXIMISE PROFIT IN NEW AND ESTABLISHED BUSINESS

A journey through business life

To Damon
Enjoy the book
Kind regards Jeremy

JEREMY RUDD

ILLUSTRATIONS BY RICHARD MAYES *Jan '18*
FOREWORD BY PROFESSOR RUTH ALLEN

To Ros, Liz, Chris and Juan – finally here it is!
You never doubted.

First published 2017

Squawk Publishing

© Jeremy Rudd, 2017

The right of Jeremy Rudd to be identified as the Author
of this work has been asserted in accordance with the
Copyright, Designs and Patents Act 1988.

British Library Cataloguing in Publication Data.
A catalogue record for this book is available from the British Library.

ISBN 978-1-999-8694-03

ABOUT THE AUTHOR

I qualified as a chartered accountant at the early age of 24 in a small practice in the north east of England. Wanting to get into the big world of industry, I joined the third largest company in the UK and a leader overseas, employing hundreds of accountants of which I was the youngest. I was an internal auditor for the midlands region, which covered over 50 locations from Poole in the south to Shipley in the north. It was an eye opener. For the first time I got to walk around huge manufacturing facilities interpreting what I saw on the factory floor and reconciling them with the dull numbers and reports sent to head office. I wanted to influence management into improving performance but was very quickly told, "That's not your job." I think the final straw was when I audited one factory in a very industrial area. I used to trudge through the factory to get a weak watery coffee from the vending machine and curse that we all had to pay for the privilege. My next assignment was the social club at the new state of the art, open-plan head office in the south where one of the cost lines was the provision of free freshly ground coffee for all staff. It was incongruous to me that this cost was the equivalent to a year's profit at the factory I had just audited. So when lying in bed one Sunday morning reading the *Sunday Times* jobs section (yes, that's how we found out about job opportunities in those days), I saw an advert for a management consultant with one of the oldest firms in that profession. It was a generalist with a product called EMU (Effective Material Utilisation) actually implementing their recommendations with a hands-on approach, not just writing a report and running away. I was honoured because they didn't employ accountants but people who could actually 'do' things. Yet they had faith in me and, as they say, the rest is history.

I have spent many years in many different countries across Europe, Africa and America in many different sectors doing what my father did – loving business, but in particular just wanting to help.

I hope I pass this on to you in the book: how to love and understand business in the way I do.

In the book I talk about the importance of having mentors, coaches, facilitators; indeed a Grandpa or a Squawk. Contact us at squawk@4magicsteps.com to bounce off any ideas; we would love to help.

Jeremy Rudd
September 2017

CONTENTS

FOREWORD

Even the most experienced person benefits from going 'back to basics' from time to time in whatever they do....

Back in the early 1990s as a young and newly-appointed manager in an innovative engineering consultancy company, I recall the pain of trying to get my head around the profitability of our projects. As a chartered civil engineer, I really enjoyed the technical challenges of our work, I had a real passion for the people side of things and especially liked developing creative solutions to projects to thrill our clients. I had done well with all of this, so my company had promoted me to a managerial position. I was very excited to have been given this opportunity at a time when young women did not often get such a chance, so I was keen to learn and to do a good job. Poring over my department's management accounts at home in the evenings in order to get up to speed as soon as possible, I struggled to identify the important data to focus on. If only *4 Magic Steps to: Double Profit* had been around then, my learning curve might have been shorter and less painful.

Fast forward a number of years and I now find I have spent almost 40 years working, delivering consultancy services to regulated and private infrastructure businesses worldwide. For at least 30 of those years I have had responsibility for profitability as a manager, director or chief executive. Through these years I have managed and grown both small and larger companies through good as well as difficult trading circumstances and learned the importance of 'knowing and understanding my numbers'. I started my current business in 2008 at the onset of the deepest recession in the UK since the war. Growing fairly rapidly through that meant keeping an exceedingly close eye on some very small but very important figures.

As you grow a business and introduce it to prospective clients, you are often asked how many staff you have and what your turnover is – big numbers always seem to go down well. Interestingly, this says nothing much about the health and sustainability of the business. Rising profit margins, a healthy cash flow and demonstrable growth in earnings are much better indicators. Equally, as a business owner or director, you may perceive that your company is running along efficiently and that you are doing as well as you can – and you might be correct. But, again, robust numbers and the right robust numbers are the only way to really ascertain your business's financial health.

With this range of experiences then, I was excited to see what Jeremy Rudd had written in his book. As a business guru who has advised companies all over the world, Jeremy has an incisive instinct to be able to home in on the 'uncomfortable' issues in any business at great speed and with canny accuracy. My personal interactions with Jeremy have been around buying and selling businesses. Before you meet Jeremy, you might think that you 'know and understand your numbers', but within five minutes of starting your discussion with him, it is soon apparent that Jeremy possibly understands them better!

I recall my first meeting with Jeremy sitting at a table opposite him, somewhere in the Cotswolds, drinking a nice coffee in a plush hotel, talking about my business with my usual energy and enthusiasm. Jeremy sat quietly taking it all in and then started to ask questions. Suddenly the room felt a lot warmer and things that I thought were clear and certain and on which I had all the detail at my fingertips became less clear and uncertain and quite challengeable. What? How does he do that? How could he home in on important business angles in such a short space of time? It's important to say that that meeting had a number of happy outcomes; one of which was getting to know Jeremy and being able to appreciate and gain benefits from the clear business mind and real focus that he has.

In *4 Magic steps to: Double Profit*, Jeremy demonstrates this focus and clarity. Through the telling of a charming and clear story he takes us 'back to basics' as we hear how an entrepreneurial young girl called Jo builds her first business with help from her Grandpa. We learn from Jo's mistakes and her Grandpa's wisdom.

As I started to read the book I initially found myself nodding sagely at the learning points and advice. As I progressed through the book the nodding stopped and was replaced by some brow furrowing as I needed to concentrate harder. The nodding and furrowing was then replaced by some 'Oh, yes!' sort of 'light bulb' moments, followed by the picking up of a pencil and making notes of thoughts and ideas for my own use. The engaging story in the book makes the business messages clear and memorable – especially as the business coach is a muscular big bird called Squawk. As Jo starts to develop her business selling apples, she and the readers are introduced to a set of simple tools – the 4 MAGIC STEPS – which focus on the important impact of price, sales, costs and fixed costs on profit and cash in a business. We learn with Jo as her business starts to become more complex.

Going back to basics is always a good thing no matter how experienced we are and, in fact, some of the best advice is common sense – something we all need reminding of from time to time. Jeremy brings common sense, practical examples and punchy learning points together and inspires you to take action in the way he has inspired businesses to grow and improve all over the world.

I previously commented that I have a real passion for 'the people side of things'. I have spent a lot of time in my career enthusiastically helping to develop young engineers and entrepreneurs. Through my role as National Chair of the Pipeline Industries Guild, I initiated and established a UK/Ireland Young Professionals Network to support young people in developing their careers in the oil, gas, water and telecom sectors. It's often too easy to focus on technical training and development in these areas and omit the business coaching which is an important component for this network. Equally, as the Royal Academy of Engineering Visiting Professor of Infrastructure at Exeter University, I am keen that the Engineering, Maths and Physical Sciences Faculty includes business coaching for its aspiring technical graduates. Anyone who works with young people will have benefited from the energy and enthusiasm that they emanate. It's a delightful privilege to be able to do this. As such, introducing tomorrow's business leaders to good advice and clear thinking at an early stage in their development is an important thing to do. They would do well to read about the 4 MAGIC STEPS and I am certain that they would take on the learning points and concepts and benefit from them as quickly as Jo does in the book.

Reading about the 4 MAGIC STEPS has taken me 'back to basics' and refreshed my focus on profit and service. Selling consultancy advice, as my business does, is different to selling apples, which is where Jo starts. However, the focus on getting sales to make a profit to generate cash is the same in any business... and who wouldn't want to double their profits?

Professor Ruth Allen
Malmesbury
September 2017

INTRODUCTION:
WHO SHOULD READ THIS BOOK

The simple answer is: if you care about your business you should read this book.

You should read this book if you have ever wanted to set up a new business but are nervous about the risks. Remember you had that wonderful idea for a product or service you could offer but it got shelved because it felt too difficult to start a business?

You should also read this book if you care about profit. Many businesses lose sight of this critical objective, so if you are running a business and are anxious that it's not making enough profit, get your whole team to read this book.

I have helped clients in Europe, Africa and America over many years and I have seen many techniques for profit improvement, but they all come back to 4 MAGIC STEPS that really work, and quickly.

Maybe your business suffers from corporate blindness – a sort of tunnel vision? Teams may be achieving defined objectives in disparate parts of the business, but how do these relate to profit? It is surprising that many managers and executives are motivated by something other than profit and don't know where they fit in to deliver what the company needs. Do your sales teams worry about profit or just getting the next sale? Do they have the right objectives? Do you know why all parts of the business exist? Do your customers value them? What is their economic activity?

Throughout this book I focus on cash. This is because all businesses, whether a local hairdresser or international healthcare conglomerate, have the same focus: making a profit to generate cash. Cash is the lifeblood of any business. Sales are often the focus as the test for the health of a business, but as we see in Jo's story, cash is the reality.

Cash is relevant to all organisations, including 'not for profit' organisations such as the NHS, charities or even schools, where cash surplus/deficit is monitored closely and used as the scoreboard.

These 'not for profit' organisations are the same as any other business. The management's duty is to run the organisation efficiently without waste, and to identify which economic activities consume or generate optimum levels of cash.

Every organisation has some activities that are no longer relevant or indeed not wanted by their customers, but they have become overlooked in time.

They are run diligently by dedicated people, but they are not adding value.

This book shows the birth of a new business and will teach you step by step how to make sustainable profits. These lessons can also be adopted by established businesses to substantially improve their profits.

This book will:

- Show methods to succeed when setting up a business.
- Guide you to make more profit.
- Illustrate how to set the right price to optimise your product profitability.
- Give tips to increase sales volume.
- Show how to cut your cost base and how greater efficiency can have an impact on profit without affecting customer satisfaction.
- Discuss why fixed costs are so sticky and are the enemy of profit, especially in a low-margin business.
- Identify why time is so important to making profit.

But the main focus of this book are the 4 MAGIC STEPS.

So let's go and find more cash!

THE JOURNEY

Jo was enjoying a busy afternoon on her paper round, delivering the local newspaper to more houses than usual. She had just taken over another round so was working twice as hard for the same cash. She only had her teddy bear to keep her company. Sitting on the handle bars, Mr Ted's eyes were on her all the time.

Jo was happy because the sun was shining and she was making cash, but she was sad because she wanted to run her OWN business. She just knew she could run a business better than her boss ran his, make more cash AND be her own boss, but she was scared to try.

Jo was going past her grandfather's house, so she thought she would stop and have a break as her legs ached from all the cycling. She sat by the house watching the little stream running down the road next to her. It was so nice with the sun warming her. She lay down on the grass, closed her eyes and went into a deep sleep.

Startled, Jo suddenly sat up. Mr Ted was sitting next to her, leaning on her legs and eating a big apple, the juice dripping off his chin. He looked at Jo and asked,

"Do you want a bit? It is delicious."

Jo took a big bite and wondered where it had come from.

"It's free; I got it from Grandpa's orchard. There are lots, go and help yourself – but leave plenty for me!" Mr Ted laughed.

As Jo was eating her delicious apple Mr Ted said, "Here is the business you wanted! You could sell these apples and make a lot of cash. What do you think?"

Jo thought it a great idea, but told him that it was his idea so she needed to make him a partner to help her. Mr Ted quickly agreed, thinking about all the cash he would make.

"That's great, Mr Ted. I do need you because
I would be scared to do it by myself. I don't know what
to do – it's a risk because I have to give up my job."
Jo thought carefully. "I'll do it – I will set up my stall
tomorrow. But first we need to talk to Grandpa."Jo
was so excited she rushed up the garden path, but
suddenly became overcome by nerves. Mr Ted had to
push her.

Grandpa must have seen them because he was
waiting at the door.

Jo said nervously, "Mr Ted and I have a wonderful idea for a business for me – I can stand at your gate and sell lots of apples from your orchard!" Grandpa frowned. "Why do you want to do that? What about your job?" he asked.

"I want my own business and to make lots of cash. I will give the paper round up. Really, Grandpa, it only pays small amounts of cash. Mr Ted says I only have to sell a box of apples a week and I will be laughing with all the cash jingling in my pockets."

Mr Ted was hiding behind Jo's back but pushing her forward.

Grandpa wanted to encourage Jo, but he also wanted her to learn, so he told her, "Jo, this is a risk. Remember at the moment you get cash for your job, day in, day out. You will lose this regular cash in your pocket.

"Make a target, Jo. Be sure, for instance, that you will make more cash than in your current job. After all, you will be very miserable if you don't make enough cash.

"All businesses must have clear targets!" he shouted to her as she left. "Remember: no target, no success. Come back to me tomorrow to tell me how you get on."

After Jo had finished talking with Grandpa about what she was going to do she went to the orchard and got busy, picking all the apples and putting them away safely. Grandpa had said they must be kept in the dark, not too close to each other.

It was fun and exciting; she was finally her own boss, the start of something new.

Jo polished and wrapped each apple lovingly. It was hard work and took many hours until she became exhausted, but her store was full of boxes of apples at the end. Mr Ted came along and laughed at all her hard work.

"You are wasting time – just throw them into a box," he laughed.

"We must make our target, and having the best apples will help," she rebuked him.

Jo put up a stall and laid out her shiny apples, but as she made signs for her stall she suddenly wondered what price to charge for the apples. She didn't worry too much and just decided to see how much her customers would give her, and anyway, Mr Ted had gone to sleep in the warm sunshine so she could not ask him.

When Mr Ted woke he saw that Jo was very busy with customers, who were buying lots of apples.

"That's good," he thought, and turned over and went back to sleep again. He didn't feel Jo shaking him, trying to wake him up.

As the sun went down Mr Ted woke up again. He saw that the stall had been taken down and that Jo was about to go home. He smiled at Jo and said, "You must have done well! You have sold all your apples."

Jo was still on a high from having so many customers and selling all her apples, but she said "Yes, but I wanted your help. You promised you would. I needed another box of apples from the store as I sold out. Anyway, here is your share of the cash as agreed; I'm off to see Grandpa."

SAVE ME

Grandpa greeted Jo with a big smile. "How was your day?" he asked.

Jo didn't know what to say, but nervously explained, "Well, Grandpa, I enjoyed myself. It was busy and exciting not having a boss, and my new customers were very nice, but I don't have as much cash in my pocket as I normally do."

Suddenly she was downcast. "What did I do wrong? SAVE ME, Grandpa."

Grandpa sat for a while before saying, "I think you have learnt a lot today. Businesses sometimes are too busy to work out what to do properly before they set off, and that was your mistake too."

Grandpa stood up and asked, "Remember we talked about a target? What was it?"

Jo remembered. "I promised to have more cash in my pocket at the end of the day than I normally do."

"So, Jo," Grandpa said "Pick up the iPad and list what happened today."

Grandpa watched the screen on the wall as Jo wrote:

- Target missed, not enough cash made.
- Too busy.
- Had fun.
- Lots of nice customers.
- Customers took advantage of me.
- All apples sold.
- Could have sold more.
- After giving Mr Ted his wages I didn't have enough cash in my pocket at the end of the day to meet my target.

At that moment a big scary bird flew in through the window, squawking loudly, and landed on Grandpa's sofa. Jo jumped up, frightened, but Grandpa said, "Don't worry about Squawk, I've worked with him for many years. As you can see, he has fought his way to many victories in business."

Jo saw the sticking plaster and wooden leg and realised how much experience he had.

Grandpa continued, "I asked him to come and help."

Squawk squawked, "I was flying around watching you sell your apples. I could see customers grabbing lots of apples but not paying much cash. It is easy to sell things cheap, but that way you will always be a busy fool and will never make lots of cash."

Frowning, he looked at the screen on the wall and said, "Jo, let's look at each of these points, but first remind me: why did you start your own business?"

Remembering her conversation with Grandpa, Jo knew what Squawk was aiming for. "To have more cash in my pocket than normal," she said confidently, but she was surprised when Squawk continued.

"And how were you planning to do that?' he queried.

"By selling lots of apples, of course," replied Jo indignantly.

Squawk laughed. "But you did that today and made less. Why?"

Now Jo was wondering what went wrong. She hadn't thought about it before but it dawned on her that she didn't have a plan to achieve her cash target. How did she know how many apples to sell if she

hadn't worked out a price?

She asked, "Was it because I didn't know how many to sell at the right price?"

"Eureka!" shouted Squawk. "Now list what must be done."

Grandpa stepped in and said, "Look at the screen Jo, I think we agree that the rules you have to follow to have a successful business are:

1. Always have a TARGET

"Neither entrepreneurs nor executives have focus unless they have targets.
And you can only make target with a plan."

He wrote on the screen:

NO TARGET, NO SUCCESS

2. Agree a PLAN

"Make a plan of how you are going to make your target cash by selling enough apples at a price you choose."

He added to the screen:

NO PLAN, NO TARGET

3. Choose and fix your PRICE

"What price should you charge, and how do you work that out? It is not simple to know what price to charge – you have to do some research about who your customers will be and what they will pay. But you also must understand your costs.

"Do your research to work out your price then see how many apples you have to sell to make your target."

NO PRICE, NO PLAN

went on the list.

"Your research must find out two things: first, before you start selling you should know the market. Who are your prospective customers? Why do they want your apples? How much do they pay at the moment? How do they VALUE your apples – do they love them? In other words, how much are they prepared to pay?

"The second is COST. Before you set a price you must understand how much each apple costs – it is no good setting a price less than cost."

Grandpa added the fourth and final point on the list:

NO RESEARCH, NO PRICE

Grandpa said, "So, Jo, sit down with Mr Ted and work out what to do next."

Jo quickly wrote down her action points:

Succeed By Agreeing a

Target
Plan   -   Price
           -    Volume

Using Research
           -    Value (Market)
           -    Cost (Internal)

Jo was happy she knew what she had to do and was just leaving when Grandpa said, "I want to make sure you don't forget the lesson of knowing how to price your apples and that they are not free, so I am going to charge you for them.

"I will charge you 10p for each apple, so that's the first cost you have to cover. Let's have a review meeting again tomorrow to make sure we have got it right."

"Thank you, Grandpa and Squawk, you have given me lots of advice to SAVE ME, which will help me remember what to do!"

Jo went off to tell Mr Ted what she had learned; she was exhausted but wanted to explain everything.

Mr Ted sat looking at Jo and laughed when he heard that Grandpa was charging her for the apples.

"Grandpa is going to get richer than you!" he giggled. But he listened to Jo as she explained what she had learnt.

"No, seriously, Mr Ted, today we learnt that pricing is the first step to success – without getting it right all our planning fails.

"Mr Ted, I asked Grandpa to SAVE ME when I could not work out why there wasn't enough cash. SAVE ME is what we need to do!

Set a target for what we want to achieve.
Agree a plan to achieve our target.
Value our product – do market research to see how much our customers value it so that we know the optimum price to charge.
Explore the cost of our product, find out all the costs and taking this and the market

research into account price our product
correctly.

And then afterwards:

Measure & analyse the outcome.
Explain the outcome with our team and
Grandpa and use any lessons to make
tomorrow more successful."

Jo was determined her business would work, so she
decided she would get there earlier and work later
to make sure she had lots of cash at the end of the
day. She also talked with Mr Ted about what went
wrong. She wanted a plan ending up with lots of cash
jingling in her pocket.

MAGIC STEP 1

Now that she had learnt how to price her product, Jo took charge.

"Mr Ted, you need to research to see what VALUE people put on what we sell. Go round all the shops in the area and find out how much they charge for their apples; whilst you are there talk with the customers and ask them what would make them buy from us. You shouldn't be afraid of our customers," Jo added, "we have a wonderful product: the apples taste great, shine beautifully, are locally grown and not transported across the world. Off you go around all the local shops to see how much they are charging for their apples whilst I am polishing more apples for tomorrow.

"But first let's work out our costs. Let's aim to sell a box of apples a day. There are 100 apples in each box. We know Grandpa is charging us 1,000p for them, but what about the other things we need to cover?"

Mr Ted quickly said, "Well, we need to add the same amount of cash that you used to get from work – that's 500p, and of course there is my 500p as well."

Jo was thinking hard. "I wonder if we should put on something for profit/surplus cash?" she asked Mr Ted.

"Well, I think Grandpa would be very pleased if you did," replied Mr Ted.

So they agreed to add on 100p (5%) for profit, making a total of 2,100p. Jo scribbled it down to make sure they were right.

For 100 apples

Apples	1000
Jo	500
Ted	500
Profit	100
Selling price	21p

"So, Mr Ted, our selling price for each apple is 21p.

"Right, you go off and find out how much the shops are charging. See if there is anything the customers may want which would add to the value they place on our apples, and if there is anything we could do to help them."

Mr Ted did his work diligently. Going to lots of shops – 'our competitors' Jo had reminded him – he looked at their range of apples, spoke to a lot of people and found there were a lot of ways they could be different from the other shops. He went back to Jo and gave her the news.

"Jo, we could actually charge more than we thought, if we added value. Here are some of the customers' ideas. We will have happy customers if we:

- Had the shiniest apples.
- Wrapped them in paper.
- Went round each customer to see how many they wanted each week.
- Delivered the apples to their house.
- Gave away special recipe sheets, different ones each week for apple crumble, cake and other delicacies.
- Sliced them up into easy to eat chunks."

They agreed to try all of these ideas, and they were also confident enough to raise their selling price to 22p.

Jo revised her pricing calculations, and she quickly worked out they would DOUBLE their profit by putting their price up by just 5%!

Jo was really pleased with Mr Ted's research and immediately revised her signs to 22p.

"This is a big step," said Jo.

SHOCK
SURPRISE

For 100 apples

Apples	1000
Jo	500
Ted	500
Profit	200
Selling price	22p

In fact, Jo and Mr Ted had stumbled upon MAGIC
STEP 1:

MAGIC STEP 1:
Even small changes in the price you
charge for your product/services can
make a HUGE difference to your profit

Profit dramatically changes when you optimise
your price, and just a 5% increase in price meant a
doubling of profit for Jo.

Jo and Mr Ted didn't see Squawk swooping down past
them into Grandpa's. He landed on Grandpa's sofa
and said, "You won't believe your little team has just
worked out the most powerful and quickest way of
increasing profit! They have found out the dramatic
relationship between the selling price and profit,

that a 5% increase in price DOUBLES their profit. Increasing price is always dramatic, because your costs don't move. Depending on your margin you can increase profit significantly."

Squawk drew a simple chart. He wanted everyone to understand how important it was.

Impact of Increasing Selling Price

Price INCREASE	Existing Margin			
	5%	10%	20%	25%
	PROFIT WILL INCREASE BY:			
2%	40%	20%	10%	8%
5%	100%	50%	25%	20%
10%		100%	50%	40%
15%			75%	60%
20%			100%	80%
25%				100%

"Businesses that have a 5% margin like Jo's will see their profit DOUBLE with a 5% increase in price. Even a business with a 20% margin will increase profit by 25% if it increases prices by 5%."

SQUAWK'S ACTION POINTS FOR ALL BUSINESSES:
MAGIC STEP 1: OPTIMISING PRICE

- **Always get the last %.** Ask yourself: "If we increased our prices by 1% would we lose that sale?" The answer is probably no. What about 5%? 10%? More? If this is not being done you are losing profit. Few sales teams are rewarded on margin – more likely their bonus is based on how much they sell rather than the profit they have created, and of course it is easier to close a deal at a lower price. But as we can see in the table above, even small increases in price have a huge impact on the bottom line.

- **Review prices regularly.** Don't put it off because it is difficult, and don't be afraid to put the price up. If you have a premium product you don't need to beat the competitors' price. A higher price gives confidence. If you had a ground-breaking piece of technology and only charged 10% of the price of a rival then customers may question the quality of the product. It's all about whether the customer senses value.

- **Find out what your customers value.** Previously people wanted their purchase to work and be cheap, like Ford's Model T car. But that's not the focus any more. A product has to be the best, the sleekest, the fastest, the greenest, the easiest to use, the most fashionable and available immediately. Price is now not always top of the list.

- **Understand the direct value of your customers to the business.** Be aware of how price sensitive they are and their loyalty. Reward them. Remember, it is likely that 20% of your customers will generate 80% of your profit.

- **Let unprofitable customers go.** At the other end of the profitability list are customers who regularly moan about price, constantly call to complain and consume the energy of your business. Let them go – they are costing you money. At a packaging factory in Africa we discovered that 95% of the net profit was made from only 20% of the customers. By culling the unprofitable ones the company ended up a highly profitable, nimble and customer-focused leader of the industry.

MAGIC STEP 2

The next day Jo persuaded Mr Ted to use her bike to go round the village visiting new and old customers. He would ask them how many apples they wanted and then he would deliver the apples on a Friday.

Jo worked on keeping the apples polished and wrapped nicely. Sometimes, when she had time, she sliced up apples for Mr Ted to deliver to customers. She also got her Mum to make up some recipes to hand out to her regular customers for them to use to make lovely apple cake and other delicacies.

Jo worked out who were her top 10 customers and sometimes she gave them some spices with the recipes to make them feel special.

Each time she went back to Grandpa with her report he was delighted with her progress.

One day he even surprised her when he analysed her cash surplus, because not only had they doubled profit by charging 22p, but on average they had sold 105 apples a day. With this 5% increase their profit had gone up again!

Jo was delighted and, thinking about how a 5% increase in price had DOUBLED her profit, she said, "So have we doubled our profit again Grandpa?"

"I like your thinking, Jo, but this impact to your business is not as great as putting up price. When you put up your price, each and every apple you sell means ALL the extra cash is yours because your costs don't go up.

"It is different when you sell extra because you are only adding cash before paying your supplier (me) for the apple. So in this case you are selling them at 22p and paying me 10p so the net effect is that you get 12p to keep.

"Each day you are selling an extra 5 apples. 10p each still goes to me and you keep 12p each, making 60p extra each day. So your profit goes up from 200p to 260p – an increase of 30%, which is amazing as well."

Grandpa got the iPad and wrote:

- Profit quickly moves when sales go up or down.
- Jo's profit increased by 30% when sales went up 5%.

Squawk had flown in and, standing on the window ledge, said "Jo, Grandpa has shown you MAGIC STEP 2. Make sure you follow this advice."

MAGIC STEP 2:
Changes in the volume of your sales quickly affect your profit

SQUAWK'S ACTION POINTS FOR ALL BUSINESSES:
MAGIC STEP 2: INCREASING SALES

- **Make it easy for your customers to get what they want immediately.** Customers take a lot of time researching but once they have decided to buy your product they want it now.

- **Don't be misled – how much your product costs to make is not important to the customer.** In the buying process people assess price on what THEY will gain or lose; price is what the market can bear.

- **Always give options.** Offer a 'light' version for those with a tight budget, and at the other end offer extras to improve 'sensed' value. I had an ice cream round in my school holidays. Having small cones satisfied the customers with little cash but I also made sure there was plenty to add onto my basic 'Mr Whippy', such as chocolate sauce and ground almonds, to get my price up, and of course my margin increased dramatically. It almost paid you to give them to the first customer, as the customers behind in the queue were always tempted!

- **Always spoil your loyal customers**. Never forget the people who have bought from you before: it means they trust you and are willing to give you money. Think of all that money you will save from trying to get new customers on board.

- **Add value**. My father had a newsagent/tobacconist in a resort town. In his product range he had matches and postcards, and one quiet day he took a postcard and stuck it on a matchbox, put it on the counter at double the price of the original items and it immediately sold as a souvenir. This range turned out to be his biggest profit earner.

- **Offer bundles.** If you are a hairdresser, for instance, offer to add in a bottle of shampoo at a discount if customers come in on your quiet time.

- **The customer is king, but fickle.** Never rest on your laurels. Your product will never last forever; price will always be challenged. Innovate, experiment and keep asking them what they want. Listen to their answers or your business will die. Did you know that 60% of the businesses in the FTSE 100 initial index in the 1980s do not still exist?

"But in going after all these lovely sales, make sure you don't forget MAGIC STEP 1."

MAGIC STEP 1:
Even small changes in the price you charge for your product/services can make a HUGE difference to your profit

"Just as a small increase to your selling price has a huge impact on your profit, so does a small decrease, because your costs are still the same. Remember never to lower your price to get extra sales unless you have some reduced cost to pass on.

"If price is reduced in a sale for example, you will have to work really hard to keep your profit. Depending on your gross margin, a small change to your pricing strategy will have a dramatic impact on your profit. If you have a 5% margin, a price reduction of just 2% means you have to sell 67% more products to get the same profit. Even a business with a 25% margin has to sell 67% more if it reduces price by 10%!"

The impact of reducing your selling price:

Impact of reducing Selling Price
Your Existing Margin

Price reduction	5%	10%	20%	25%
	YOU MUST INCREASE SALES BY:			
2%	67%	25%	11%	9%
5%		100%	33%	25%
10%			100%	67%
15%			300%	150%
20%				400%

"Come and see me if you are even thinking of reducing your price," Squawk growled to Jo before flying off.

MAGIC STEP 3

Jo woke up having a panic attack. Yesterday she and
Mr Ted had introduced a new product: a chocolate
apple flapjack biscuit that they made themselves.
But instead of making her usual 200p profit she had
lost 920p! How? Where did all the cash go? Why did
it happen? How can she sort it out before she loses
everything?

Her mind went back to the beginning.

Mr Ted had been getting bored with just selling apples
and he thought their customers were bored too:
sales had fallen back to 2,200p a day on average. Of
course, they were still making 200p on a daily basis,
but he just felt they had to DO something. He had
collared Jo to explain his thoughts.

So when Jo was having her daily meeting with
Grandpa she had asked if he thought it a good idea to
make something to sell alongside the apples.

He said, "Yes, remember Squawk's notes? It's a
good idea to keep looking for ways to add value and
have something new for your customers. But you

must be focused. Don't lose sight of the successful business you have now – do it to increase your profit, not just because Mr Ted is bored."

Grandpa was worried that Jo and Mr Ted did not have any experience of making things, so he said sternly, "Make sure you understand all the economic activities involved, count the cash carefully and report back to me."

Jo was confused. "What are economic activities, Grandpa?"

He replied, "Everything you do in business is an economic activity. For instance, picking apples, buying things and making things are all examples of economic activities."

Jo thought she knew what Grandpa meant and went to find Mr Ted. Mr Ted was at home in Grandpa's old garden shed, keeping warm. "Come in, Jo, let's have a cup of tea. Meet my new friend, Debra. She cleans my home; she wants to meet you." Round the corner came a very friendly looking dormouse with a cloth in one hand and a brush in the other.

"You look busy," Jo said.

Debra replied, 'I'll be finished soon – do you need any helpers? I can do most things."

Jo said she would love to have Debra as part of the team. She then explained she had talked to Grandpa about Mr Ted's idea about making some products to sell alongside the apples. "What do you think the customers would like?" she asked.

Mr Ted said, "I've been thinking about this. Your Mum makes those amazing flapjacks – could we sell them? Or chocolate. People love eating chocolate, so let's sell it!" he said dreamily.

Jo liked the idea but knew that chocolate was very expensive and was worried. "We cannot just buy and sell chocolate, Mr Ted – everybody does that. We have to be different."

"Eureka!" Mr Ted shouted. "I'm thinking chocolate, apples, and flapjacks... so let's make chocolate apple flapjack biscuits!"

"That's an amazing idea, Mr Ted," Jo continued, "We can make them in Mum's kitchen."

Mr Ted said excitedly "Really? Do we really get to make chocolate biscuits?" His mouth started watering again. Jo put him right straight away. "Yes, but we will use chocolate CAREFULLY because it costs a lot of cash. Come with me. Let's look on the Internet to find out how to make them."

When they got to Mum's kitchen Jo said, "My Mum has special trays with lots of little individual moulds to make nice little chocolate biscuits. It looks like we simply put a little chocolate in, drop in the flapjacks, fill up as much of the remaining space with apple pieces and finally pour more yummy chocolate over them until we fill the moulds and scrape off any excess chocolate."

Mr Ted jumped up. "Does that mean I get to eat that wasted bit?"

Jo quickly said, "No, that goes back in to make the next one, otherwise you would get fat and we would lose all our cash." Jo could feel Squawk grinning with approval.

Then Jo remembered what she had to do before they got to work. "Come on Mr Ted, we have to work out how to SAVE ME," she said. So together they worked out what they would do and Jo wrote:

Set a target: Our target is to have at least twice as much cash when we finish.

Agree our plan of action: We agree to make biscuits following the specification in my recipe.

Value the new biscuits: Mr Ted will visit shops to work out what value the customers place on similar biscuits so we can decide what price we should charge.

Explore the cost: I will make a recipe for us to follow when making the biscuits to make sure we know how much they cost.

Measure and

Explain results: We will carefully add up the cash and report to Grandpa and, if necessary, make any changes.

Jo went to the kitchen and weighed and measured precisely a little chocolate, flapjack and some apple slices to put into the moulds. She worked out how much it cost and what to charge, and quickly scribbled it down to make sure they followed the plan. "Squawk will be pleased," she thought happily.

Costing the biscuits	
Chocolate	20.00
Flapjack	4.00
Apple slices	.40
Profit	2.60
Selling price	27p

Jo's Mum gave her precisely the right amount of chocolate she needed for 100 biscuits. Mum asked who was going to make them and Jo realised that of course she could not be in two places at once, so she asked Debra to look after the stall whilst she and Mr Ted were busy. Whilst they were all there they decided to call the biscuits 'Chocka biscuits'.

Jo gave half the chocolate to Mr Ted. They each went to get the apple slices and flapjacks that Jo had put out earlier and off they started, Jo at one end of the kitchen table and Mr Ted at the other.

Jo made her Chocka biscuits carefully, putting in the first layer of chocolate then placing the flapjacks gently onto the chocolate. She added the bits of apple onto the flapjack, making sure there was only space for a little of the expensive chocolate to finish it off.

Mr Ted on the other hand was in a rush, because he had to go to the shops to work out what price to charge, so he poured in chocolate but sometimes he did not bother to put in a full flapjack or the apple slices because it was so difficult.

"I've finished!" shouted Mr Ted. "All my chocolate is gone!" Then he rushed off for a cup of tea then to the shops to check what prices everyone was charging.

Jo took her time to finish her Chockas. She was very proud of them and they all looked lovely. Whilst she tidied up she was a little surprised that there were some flapjacks and apple slices left over, and lots of crumbs with chocolate splashed around on Mr Ted's side. "I must tell him off," she thought angrily, "We can't make a mess in Mum's kitchen!"

Jo went to the stall to see how Debra was doing. "I hope you told the customers to come tomorrow for our lovely new delicacies," Jo asked.

Debra said she had done, but she added "I was so busy I needed to get a friend to help, because we had to deliver the apples that Mr Ted normally takes to customers. I hope I did the right thing."

Jo replied, "Well done, Debra, thanks for doing that, I have been so busy I had forgotten."

When Debra heard how busy Jo was she suggested she take the cash to her house, which was below Mr Ted's garden shed. "My sister, Sage, lives there. She is brilliant at looking after cash and has lots of different tins to put it in."

Jo was delighted with the help because she was rushing around. She couldn't keep up, and Grandpa had said she had to be vigilant with the cash.

Later, when Sage knew of her new responsibilities, she sent over two tins for the stall: one for apple cash and one for Chocka biscuits cash.

The next morning, before the stall opened, Jo made some big signs. She had taken time to work out the price to charge based on the recipe. Mr Ted said, "The prices of biscuits in the shops nearby are much higher and you could charge more." But Jo didn't want to be greedy. She was happy with a 10% profit.

"I want to be nice to our customers," she replied.

CHOCKAS

Yummy chocolate,
apple, flapjack
biscuits

Only 27p

Jo had been very excited. She and Debra worked busily all day, customers came and bought lots of the new biscuits, and even Squawk came along and bought some before everything on the stall sold. Jo was surprised how fast the Chockas had sold out – she was sure there should have been more. But there was lots of cash in the tins so she was happy.

After tidying up, they went back to Mr Ted's, and gave all the cash to Sage to sort out. Sage got busy with her tins: she had one for each cost and even had one for the profit.

Jo's Mum had told her what must be paid for the flapjacks and chocolate so Sage rushed off with two tins overflowing with cash to pay her. When she came back she put cash into Jo's and Mr Ted's tins and also into Debra's. There was even a tin for her friend who had helped her. She then got another tin for her own cash and all the rest went into Grandpa's. The pile of cash had become smaller all the time.

Finally, Sage said to Jo she must take Grandpa's cash to him. But when Jo looked into Grandpa's tin, there wasn't enough cash! She shook the profit tin: it was empty!

"Sage, you must have made a mistake," Jo said,

"Where is Grandpa's cash?"

Sage recounted, checking all her tins, but everything was correct. She had put all the cash she had been given into the right tins; there was just not enough to put into Grandpa's.

Sage gave Jo a list of the tins and their contents so Jo could see what had happened to the cash.

Jo was shocked. She couldn't believe it, but asked Sage to take out cash from her tin to make sure she had enough for Grandpa.

Jo then decided to go home and see Grandpa in the morning.

Jo came back to the present. It was not a nightmare, it had actually happened: she had lost cash yesterday. She dragged her feet as she walked up to Grandpa's house. She was a little nervous because she knew there was going to be a discussion.

Grandpa looked wisely at Jo. "So, Jo, have you brought me my cash for the apples?" he asked. "You are late coming to see me, so I assume there is a problem, because there is a saying: 'bad numbers take longer to add up.'"

"I have your cash, Grandpa, but we lost cash overall. I don't know what happened. Where is it? How can I find it?"

Jo continued. "We have been very busy making things to sell; I even worked out how much to charge for them. We checked how much to price the new biscuits, everyone loved them, and we quickly sold all we made. But at the end of the day I had to take cash out of MY tin. I don't know where it's gone. Did I lose it at the stall or walking to Mr Ted's?" She felt tears coming into her eyes.

Grandpa said, "Don't panic, it's ok, Jo. At least you know something is wrong – lots of businesses don't find out until it is too late – and you can pay all your bills, so it's not a disaster.

"We will work this out," Grandpa continued, "but we must simplify the numbers – starting with some hard facts. What did you expect to have in your profit tin today?"

Thinking back to her plan, Jo got out the iPad and wrote:

I planned to have profit (surplus cash) from:

Sale of Apples	200
Sale of Chocka biscuits	260
Total cash in surplus tins	460

Then she started to panic again as she remembered there was no cash in the profit tin. "I even had to take 460p out of my tin to put into yours, so that means in total I had a loss of 920p!"

HUGE LOSS

Expected cash	460
Jo's cash to pay Grandpa	460
TOTAL LOSS	920

"How can we have lost so much cash just by adding a new product?" Jo was in despair.

Grandpa quickly interrupted. "Jo, calm down, let's get back to basics. It's all to do with BALANCE: what comes in must go somewhere, and what goes out must have come from somewhere."

Now it was Grandpa's turn to use the iPad (which Jo found quite funny as he had to ask her how to turn it on). He wrote:

Facts:
- You planned to have 460p surplus cash (profit) at the end of the day.
- There was no profit. You even had to take 460p out of your tin to pay all your bills.
- Your shortfall on the day was 920p.

Grandpa asked Jo to read what he had written to make sure she agreed, then said, "The next step is to list what you planned to sell yesterday."

Jo grabbed the iPad, writing:

I planned to sell:

Apples	2,200
Chocka biscuits	2,700
Total sales	4,900

Jo said, "That's a lot of cash, Grandpa. I thought we would have lots and lots left in our profit tin!"

Grandpa said, "To get a balance we need to know how much cash ACTUALLY came in from your customers compared to how much you expected, so please go and get Sage and all the tins of cash so we can work it out.

"This is really good," he encouraged her, "you clearly had a plan and that's where we have to start from. You were sensible to have Sage to help you because we will be able to find out, by looking in the tins, what has happened. Well done so far!" And he added to the lists of facts:

You planned to have total sales of 4,900p.

After Jo left, Grandpa went to his cupboard and pulled out a huge set of scales and laid them out on the floor.

When Jo and Sage were back Grandpa explained that he was going to show them how to get the numbers BALANCED and, pointing out the scales, he said, "Starting with the apples business, take all the tins of cash you have to pay out onto the right side of the scale."

Jo thought this was easy because she had seen it every day. She knew she had to pay Grandpa 1,000p and Mr Ted and herself 500p each, which was a total of 2,000p, but when she put it onto the scales it crashed to the floor on the right-hand side.

Now Grandpa went to his safe and got out 2,200p of his cash. "This cash represents the cash your customers paid for apples," he said, putting it on the left-hand side of the scales. This made his side touch the floor.

"How do we get it to balance, Jo?" he asked.

Jo scratched her head. What had she left out?

Sage was jumping up and down, whispering to Jo. "I think you have to put 200p on the right-hand side to make it balance. That is the profit we expected!"

Jo asked Sage to get the tin marked 'apples profit', and put it on the right-hand side of the scales. Now everything balanced!

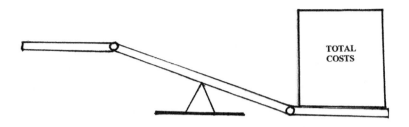

Jo puts the cash to pay Grandpa, Mr Ted and herself
onto the scales

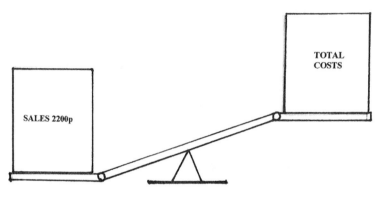

Grandpa puts on the cash from customers

Jo puts the profit on the scales – it balances

"That's it," Grandpa said with approval, "You have got the balance. Now you are in balance on the apples business." Then he got out the iPad and added another fact:

- The apples business balances. Cash from customers balances with the costs and profit as planned. The customers' cash is used to pay the bills, and 200p surplus cash is left in the tin.

"Well done, team, now we are making progress," Grandpa told them. "Now let's do the same for the expected outcome for Chocka biscuits."

Jo and Sage were quick to put all the tins with outgoings for chocolate (2,000p), flapjacks (400p) and apples (40p) and their planned profit of 260p on the right-hand side. Sage asked Grandpa if she could get cash out of his safe to balance the scales using 2,700p of Grandpa's cash for sales of 100 Chockas at 27p.

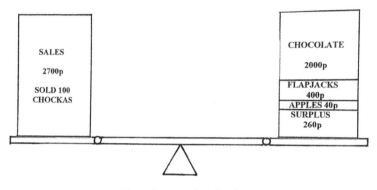

Chocka scales balance!

Grandpa quickly saw that Jo was expecting to sell 100 Chocka biscuits and have 260p in the profit tin, and adding this to the 200p surplus from the apples business meant that they should have had 460p surplus in total.

"So where did we lose the cash, Grandpa?" asked Jo. "We know it wasn't from the apples business, so it must be from the Chocka biscuits, mustn't it?"

Grandpa wanted this to be a learning experience for Jo and her team and replied, "Jo, go to your team, explain you have lost cash and see what ideas they have. Remember a few things:

- The business needs to balance.

- The apples business seems ok so focus on what you did differently this time.

- Review the ingredients you bought. Did you use them efficiently? Make sure you used your ingredients effectively in line with the recipe you designed to make and price the Chocka biscuits. Then think about the huge difference in the cost of the ingredients. For the same amount you pay for chocolate you could get 50 apple slices or 5 flapjacks. Chocolate is precious, it has a lot more value. Was it used carefully?

- Your recipe was precise about the ingredients to use to make a Chocka biscuit. You specified how much chocolate, flapjacks and apple you were going to use to make one. You had exactly enough chocolate for 100 Chocka biscuits. Do you think you made 100 perfect Chocka biscuits? Do you think the chocolate got lost in the kitchen?

- Are you sure Sage got all the cash the customers gave you?

- Are there any tins still in Sage's house?

- Are there any more costs you hadn't planned?"

Squawk suddenly flew in through the window. "Hello, Grandpa," he said. "I think they need me to go with them to help, but first I'll let them make a start whilst you and I have a catch up."

Jo and Sage went back to Mr Ted's, where all the team were having a cup of tea. Jo explained that instead of having 460p in the profit tin there was none and she had had to take 460p out of her tin to pay Grandpa. "This means we have lost 920p," she said.

Jo looked around the team and asked, "Does anybody know where it is? Have any of you any ideas where we should start looking?"

They started debating and came up with some ideas:

- Was cash stolen or lost?
- Were Chocka biscuits stolen or did we eat them?
- Did we leave anything in the kitchen?
- Is there a hole in the floor in the kitchen where chocolate got lost?
- Did anything fall under the stall?
- Did Jo drop the cash in the garden between the stall and Mr Ted's?

Jo took charge. "Debra, you go to the kitchen and see if anything was left behind, and ask your friend who helped with apple deliveries to check around the stall and in the garden to see if anything was dropped. I will go through the tins again with Sage to make sure we understand how we are going to balance the results."

Mr Ted said he would have another cup of tea and think hard about where the cash might be.

Just as they were all getting back Squawk flew in and sat on the table looking at them. "Carry on," he said, "pretend I am not here." They all laughed nervously.

Debra's friend reported back: no cash or apples or biscuits were to be seen at the stall or in the garden. Debra said she remembered selling all the apples and

Chockas. Jo agreed: she remembered the fight for the last ones between her customers!

Debra then said, "I went to the kitchen; it is spick and span, shiny everywhere, no chocolate, no Chockas – so I went to Mum to see if she tidied them away and Mum said, 'I haven't seen any, but I do remember that when you came to collect them to take them to the stall there were 50 on Jo's tray but only 40 on Mr Ted's.'"

Squawk jumped down and said, "So you finally found out that you only made 90 Chockas but you had enough expensive chocolate to make 100. Where did it go?"

Jo suddenly remembered Grandpa's words and told the team what he had instructed her. "Make sure you used your ingredients effectively. When you wrote your recipe to make and price the Chocka biscuits think about the huge difference in the cost of the ingredients. For the same amount you pay for chocolate you could get 50 apple slices or 5 flapjacks.

Chocolate is the key ingredient as it has a lot more value. Use it carefully."

Jo worried about Mr Ted's biscuits. Why did he run out of chocolate after 40 Chockas? Why were there apple slices and bits of flapjack all over his end of the kitchen table? Jo said nervously to Squawk, "We didn't control how much chocolate we used. And it cost a lot."

"You've just found MAGIC STEP 3," replied Squawk.

MAGIC STEP 3:
Control your costs.

Not doing so can wipe out profit

Squawk then told them, "Let's look at how you made your Chockas."

"How can we do that, Squawk?" asked Jo. "We can't go back in time."

"Aha, don't underestimate clever old Squawk. I bought some biscuits, don't you remember? I bought 2 from one tray and 2 from the other. If we cut them in half we can see how they were made. Who has a sharp knife? Let's see what they look like."

Squawk carefully cut in half two biscuits from the first tray and said, "Look at these. They both look the same: lots of apple and a whole flapjack all covered nicely in chocolate.

"Jo, this looks like the ones you planned when you visualised yourself making the Chocka biscuits. You did it precisely, measuring out each ingredient perfectly. But how about Mr Ted? What do you think?"

Everyone looked around for Mr Ted but he had mysteriously vanished. Nobody saw him because he was hiding behind the door, listening.

Squawk then cut the other Chockas in half. The team looked on with shock when they saw that the first Chocka was almost all chocolate. The second one was a little better, with half a flapjack and a little slice of apple.

Jo watched nervously as Squawk dissected the biscuits. It looked like Mr Ted had not put in enough apple slices or flapjacks and he had filled up all the empty space with chocolate. So that's why he ran out of chocolate after he had only made 40 Chocka biscuits and why some apple slices and flapjacks were left on the kitchen table when he had finished.

"What does that mean, Jo?" Squawk asked. Jo looked glum when she realised.

"Well, it means if Mr Ted missed out the apple slices and flapjacks, which are cheap, and the space was filled with expensive chocolate, the customer got lots of chocolate, which is very expensive. They will have been happy but that was my cash that was disappearing."

"You learn quickly, Jo. You have got it spot on. You only sold 90 Chocka biscuits but used all the chocolate and wasted apples and flapjacks which had to be scrapped into the green bin.

"This is why MAGIC STEP 3 is so important. If you don't make your products to the planned recipe you will lose cash and/or customer satisfaction."

SQUAWK'S ACTION POINTS FOR ALL BUSINESSES:
MAGIC STEP 3: CONTROLLING COSTS

- **Keep the business in balance**. Cash slips
  away very quickly.

- **Have a detailed business plan for each aspect
  of your business**. Make sure you regularly
  monitor your performance against it.

- **Always be vigilant on your costs**. When
  did you last review all your activities and
  challenge them? You probably don't need
  20% of them. Grandpa and I once worked
  with the services division of a nationwide
  technology company. It was working within
  its cost budget BUT the business had not
  identified that the company's customers

did not value the service and weren't paying an economic price for it within their bundled price offer. For a small discount the customers were happy to forgo this service, which we closed, resulting in huge savings to the business.

- **Challenge all supply agreements.** Can the cost of your ingredients or products be bettered?

- **Keep the business simple.** Look at all your economic activities and see how can they be simplified or reduced.

- **When developing and launching a new product always review your pricing assumptions.** Either increase your price to cover extra manufacturing costs or review your manufacturing process to reduce costs. Don't assume your original plans remain in place.

- **Don't be frightened to change if things are not working.** Be prepared to make an investment to restructure your business – returns on restructuring are generally much higher than on acquiring a new businesses.

- **Do regular economic activity reviews**. Ensure all economic activities are appreciated by your customer.

- **Measure ingredients precisely against the specification for the day's production**. Do this by volume and value to keep check on variations in manufacturing efficiency and the varying cost of your materials.

Squawk suggested, "Let's go and see how to get the balance." So they all went up to Grandpa's house and when they got there Squawk said, "Look at the scales. They are still in balance according to your plan."

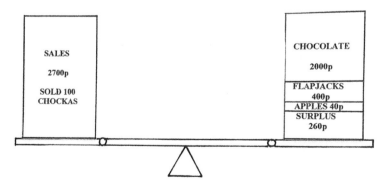

The planned balance for Chockas

"We need to understand the impact on the scales of selling 90 Chocka biscuits instead of 100," Squawk continued. "Jo, swap the 2,700p on the left-hand scale for 2,430p, which is the cash for 90 Chockas." Immediately the scales crashed to the floor on the right-hand side. "Now take off the cash for the ingredients and profit, and put them back one by one."

So Jo started by putting on 2,000p for chocolate. Nothing happened; the scales didn't move. Then she put on 400p for the flapjacks. Still nothing happened, as the right-hand scale was still in the air, but when she put on the 40p for the apples it crashed to the floor.

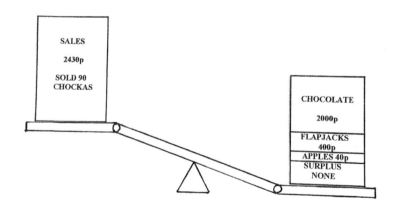

Out of balance the scales crash to the floor

Squawk reminded them that the scales had to balance. Jo said, "It won't balance if I put on the 260p for the planned profit. Sage, have you any ideas?"

Sage knew the answer. "To make it balance you have to put something on the left-hand side." So Jo slowly added 1p at a time, and when she had put 10p on the left-hand side of the scale it suddenly swung up to balance.

Instead of balancing the scales with a profit of 260p as in the plan, the costs were too heavy for the reduced sales and had to be balanced by Jo putting 10p of her own cash with the customers' cash to make sure all the bills could be paid.

Squawk summarised with another fact:

- Instead of making a profit of 260p, you had a shortfall of 10p, making a total loss against plan of 270p.

This meant that Jo had lost 270p of cash compared to what she was expecting.

Squawk continued: "We must understand what the outcome would have been if you had made and sold 90 Chockas in line with the recipe."

Squawk got Sage to leave the 2,430p – the sales value of 90 Chockas – on the left-hand scale and then one by one add the cash for the ingredients: chocolate 1,800p, flapjacks 360p and apples 36p. Finally, she put the planned profit of 234p on the right-hand scale on top of the ingredients, and the scales swung into balance.

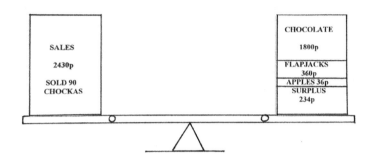

The right balance for 90 Chockas

Squawk continued: "But they were not made to specification as we know, because of Mr Ted's haphazard way of making the Chocka biscuits. This resulted in the loss of 270p.

"Jo, learn from this experience. Understanding how this loss occurred will ensure you don't do it again.

"The loss is made up of two parts: if you had made and sold 90 perfect Chocka biscuits to your specification you would have used 2,196p of ingredients, but instead you used all the ingredients, costing 2,440p to make the 90 you sold yesterday. This means you wasted ingredients worth 244p."

Squawk wrote another fact:

- Jo spent 11% (244p) too much on
  ingredients.

But you also lost the profit on the 10 Chockas that you didn't have. That's another 26p (2,700p planned sales less the planned costs of 2,440p = 260p profit/10 = 26p), making a total loss of 270p."

Squawk wrote another fact:

- Sales down by 10% lost a profit of 26p.

"Jo's excess ingredients came to 244p; the reduced sales lost her 26p, so her total shortfall was 270p. This is why it is worth remembering the MAGIC STEPS:

MAGIC STEP 3:
Control your costs.
Not doing so can wipe out profit

"By using just 11% more ingredients than in the recipe Jo's profits were down by 244p. And can you remember MAGIC STEP 2?"

    "Yes, I can," said Jo.

MAGIC STEP 2:
Changes in the volume of your sales
quickly affect your profit

Jo's sales had reduced by 10% compared to plan, and
therefore her profits fell by 26p.

Squawk flew off whilst Jo went home to try to
understand it all, but she was still worried. She now
knew why she had lost cash, but something else was
missing.

"We lost 920p," she said to
herself, confused. So off she
went to Grandpa. She knew
he would gently put her on
the right track.

When Jo asked Grandpa,
he agreed. There was still
something missing that
had consumed her cash,
because the profit from
selling her normal apples
had disappeared as well.

Grandpa wrote on the
screen:

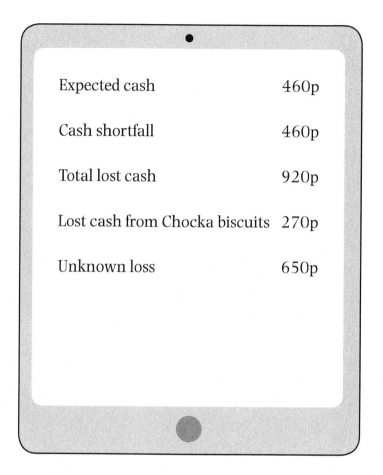

Expected cash	460p
Cash shortfall	460p
Total lost cash	920p
Lost cash from Chocka biscuits	270p
Unknown loss	650p

Grandpa asked, "Where did the rest of the cash go? Think of all the activities that were going on and see where your cash may have gone. Does each activity have a purpose? You have to be sure that your customers value each activity, because they are paying for it."

Suddenly Jo remembered all of the activities going on that were different from before. She had been so busy she hadn't thought of all the help she had called upon – it hadn't dawned on her that all the extra costs had to be paid for. The only way to do that was to charge a proper price for the Chocka biscuits, and of course to make the Chocka biscuits to the right specification in the first place.

Grandpa said, "List all the tins with cash in that Sage prepared." So Jo took out Sage's list of tins and visualised all the tins in Sage's office. She realised her cash had had to go a lot further. There were other people to pay:

Debra	350p
Debra's friend	150p
Sage	150p

All of these costs were because Jo and Mr Ted were so busy making the Chocka biscuits. Jo turned to Grandpa and said glumly, "I was so busy I forgot to update the price of Chockas to cover the extra costs I had added to the business."

"Exactly." said Grandpa. "You didn't list those extra costs when you worked out a price for the Chocka biscuits.

"Remember:

MAGIC STEP 1:
Even small changes in the price you charge for your product/services can make a HUGE difference to your profit

"Business is always changing, so make sure your prices are up to date, keeping track of any new costs. The price should have included all the costs of those involved, so what should you have set as the selling price?"

Jo got out the iPad and listed all the costs for Chockas:

Correct pricing for Chocka production

Chocolate	2,000
Apple	40
Flapjack	400
Debra	350
Debra's friend	150
Sage	150
Jo	
Ted	
Total cost	3,090
Profit	309
100	3,399
Price for 1	34

Jo said gloomily, "I should have been charging 34p but only charged 27p. No wonder I lost cash."

"Let's list what we have learned," Grandpa suggested to Jo.

Jo wrote another fact:

- I lost 7p on each Chocka we sold because I did not include all the costs when setting a selling price.

Then she wrote down all the learning experiences:

- We wasted cash because we used expensive chocolate instead of cheap apple slices and flapjacks.
- The leftover apple slices and flapjacks were wasted because they would not be fresh when we make the next batch.
- Last minute costs were forgotten and I did not include them in our pricing calculations.
- We should have charged 34p but only charged 27p, even though Mr Ted said our price was much lower than the other shops.

"But," said Grandpa, "think of the positives."

- You now know that Chocka biscuits sell well, as they sold out in an hour.
- Because of Mr Ted's research you know your customers will pay more for the Chockas.
- You know how to make them.
- Now you know that you must manage your staff to make sure that the customers don't get more chocolate than the recipe.

So the lessons learned today can be summarised in our 4 MAGIC STEPS:

MAGIC STEP 1:

Even small changes in the price you charge for your product/services can make a HUGE difference to your profit

So always know your costs when setting your price.

MAGIC STEP 2:

Changes in the volume of your sales quickly affect your profit

So be vigilant: not hitting your planned sales will reduce your profit.

MAGIC STEP 3:

Control your costs. Not doing so can wipe out profit

So make sure you make your product to your recipe/specification.

MAGIC STEP 4

"But that's only THREE MAGIC STEPS," Jo said.

"Yes," said Grandpa. To understand the 4 MAGIC STEPS you must learn something else. Remember that nobody took your cash; you gave it away. You must always be vigilant of costs. Once, Squawk and I went to Cameroon to improve the profits of a brewery. There was a crisis in the country and a lot of people couldn't afford the beer. Sales were down 30%, so we had to look at all the activities within the business to see how we could reduce costs enough to get a profit again. We first focused on fixed costs. One activity was completed by a team of employees whose job was to dispose of the used ingredients (grain, a valuable cow fodder). We got the team together and offered to set them up in business to take, sell and deliver the grain to local farmers. It was a win-win situation: they got a business with the sales and we guaranteed no cost for the grain. We got rid of an expensive fixed cost and reduced our risk.

"Now, go off, and consider how to improve your business. Look at all the activities involved, and see how they can be simplified or eradicated. Squawk will guide you."

Squawk flew in and said, "Let's get the balance right, Jo. Reassess each part of the business."

As Grandpa went off to have a cup of tea Squawk said, "Jo, let's think about the way you run the business. Is it the most efficient and lowest risk? The apple business is making 200p from sales of 2200p, but the fixed costs are 1000p so you don't make a profit until nearly 3pm in the afternoon.

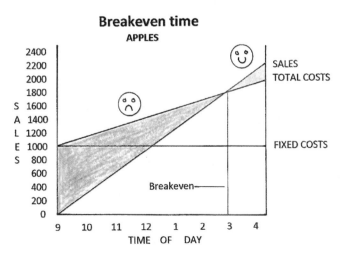

"These fixed costs are high, which means waiting until halfway through the afternoon before you start making a profit. Be aware of what happens if you sell fewer apples. For instance, if you sell 10 fewer apples you have to wait until nearly closing time before you make a profit. This shows how risky it is having high fixed costs.

"Selling 10 fewer apples means you have to wait until after 4pm before you make a profit.

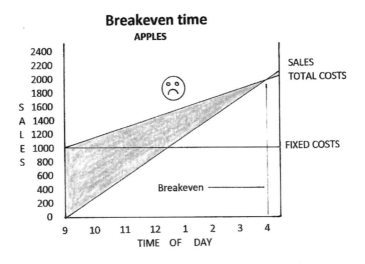

Worried until closing time!

"In business you must review all your costs, so you should do that now. For instance, you paid Debra's friend 150p for doing Mr Ted's job, but you pay him 500p. Also, is it fair that all your costs go against selling apples? What about Chockas? Remember you are very expensive. Could you make the Chockas more cheaply?"

Squawk continued. "I don't think making things is Mr Ted's forte. Perhaps get quotes for getting someone else to make the Chockas. That would reduce your risk and may be cheaper as well."

"But I don't want to fire Mr Ted," Jo said, "he's my inspiration; he is the creative one."

Squawk replied, "You must do the best for your customers and the business. But don't worry, Jo, I am not saying get rid of him – just use him to the best of his ability whilst making sure your business is run efficiently. Think about letting him remain the creative partner: allow him to stay in bed and dream, but reduce his pay to 150p. The rest can contribute to Debra and her friend's costs. He still gets 50% of all the profit, remember."

Squawk continued with his questioning. "You said that customers were being a little more cautious about buying apples, so those sales are under pressure. How can we encourage customers to still buy apples or indeed increase the sales? If we reduce the price we must reduce the cost. Have you thought of buying the apples elsewhere? I know that the neighbour has plenty to sell."

Jo was getting exhausted, but Squawk hadn't finished. "Look at all the costs – Debra did your job with ease and only charged 350p, and as she sold Chockas as well you can split that cost between apples and Chockas, 175p each.

"Her friend charged 150p for doing Mr Ted's job, so build that into your price – but don't forget that your salary is a FIXED COST and must be priced in as well. So does Mr Ted's – don't forget any costs this time!"

"So I suppose I need to add in Sage's costs too?" Jo said.

"Of course, Jo. Now that covers all the activities, and remember these fixed costs need to be covered by the profit from your products each day. If you don't sell all your Chockas one day you can sell them the next day, but your fixed costs are sticky – they have to be paid each and every day regardless of how many products you sell. Make sure you cover these costs early in the day."

Squawk told Jo to quickly reorganise the business before the morning, otherwise more cash would disappear. Then he flew off.

The first thing Jo had to do was pay Mr Ted and Debra their wages from their tins, but first she wanted to have a word with Mr Ted to tell him about the Chocka biscuits that he made and how much it cost the business. "I'm sure he will understand the implications of rushing," she thought.

After paying Debra Jo found Mr Ted in his little home lying on his bed. He looked very unhappy.

"Hey, Mr Ted, Grandpa said you had an amazing idea creating Chocka biscuits. He thinks you are clever." Mr Ted's eyes suddenly started to shine again.

"You mean I'm not in trouble?"

Jo said, "No, of course not, Mr Ted. You were the inspiration for us to do all of this. You're not in trouble, but next time we must be disciplined in how we make the Chocka biscuits, because this time we put too much chocolate in."

Mr Ted now understood what had gone wrong. "I didn't value the ingredients I was using. I didn't realise the huge price difference between each of the ingredients that went into Chocka biscuits. Now I know."

Jo admitted she got it wrong as well because she didn't include any labour costs when working out the price to charge.

"To be fair, Mr Ted," Jo added, "I admit I hadn't trained you how to make the Chockas or told you the consequences of using expensive chocolate instead of cheaper flapjacks or apple slices."

Mr Ted suddenly said, "But you know what, Jo? I am not good at that sort of thing. Why don't you get some of Debra's friends to bake the Chocka biscuits with you and I will go away and create new ideas for us?" Jo was relieved that Mr Ted suggested his move first.

Jo went to discuss making Chockas with some of Debra's friends to see if they wanted to become the Chocka mouse team, making the Chocka biscuits to her exact specification. After a while they came back to Jo, offering to make them for a fixed price of 25p each. This was based on the costs from Mum for the chocolate, flapjacks and apple slices, but they wanted a minimum order of 200 per day because they had negotiated a rebate from the chocolate supplier if Mum bought twice as much. Mum agreed to do the same with the flapjacks, and the team of mice said they would make the Chockas in their own house with their own equipment.

Jo was delighted but decided to negotiate a little. "I'll agree this price if you deliver them to the stall every morning." Everybody was happy, so they shook hands in agreement. Jo had reduced the costs and risk, as fixed costs had been converted into direct costs and saved a lot of cash and worry. But most importantly she had got rid of 6 economic activities:

- Buying chocolate.
- Buying and preparing flapjacks and apples.
- Negotiating with Mum.
- Making the Chockas.
- Cleaning the kitchen and implements.
- Delivering the Chockas to the stall.

Jo wanted to see if she could reduce the price of the apples as well, so she took Squawk's advice and went to see Grandpa's neighbour, where she negotiated a 30% reduced price compared to Grandpa. The neighbour was delighted to sell his apples and was prepared to charge 7p an apple. He would even wash and shine the apples before delivering them to the stall each morning. Importantly, Jo was able to negotiate deliveries all year round because the neighbour agreed to pick and store enough apples. Jo said she would get back to him in the morning.

SHOCK SURPRISE

She realised she had saved 5 more economic activities:

- Picking apples.
- Storing apples.
- Washing them.
- Polishing them.
- Delivering the apples to the stall.

Jo asked Squawk if she was doing the right things. He was delighted and said it was the right thing to do. "But what about Grandpa?" Jo said, "Won't he be angry I am not going to buy the apples from him?"

"Don't worry, Jo, he will be impressed that you are looking at ways to improve your business by reducing costs and economic activities. Anyway, he wouldn't want to do all of those activities and he doesn't have enough apples to supply you all year. So let's look at the new business model."

Jo was very excited to show Squawk what she had prepared with Sage. "Sage and I went through our SAVE ME routine, as we didn't want to make the same mistake as last time. I went out and negotiated new deals that would reduce our cost of ingredients and also ensured we got good quality products.

"We separated the costs into DIRECT COSTS, which vary with the quantity sold, and FIXED COSTS, which would be the same all the time regardless of whether we sold half the apples and Chockas or all of them. These are the sticky costs which include Mr Ted, Sage and myself. I now realise these costs never go away: they have to be paid each and every day."

"Well done, Jo," said Squawk, "You've found out MAGIC STEP 4."

MAGIC STEP 4:
Minimise fixed costs because they are very sticky and have to be paid every day regardless of how many items you sell

Jo smiled. "Importantly, we decided to add a 20% margin to the price because we realise now that we are taking more risks and need to build up a reserve. This means putting up the price of the Chockas, but not by as much as you would think – and they are still cheaper than the local shops."

Squawk was very impressed but he couldn't resist saying, "Jo, you are very expensive, especially as you have all these new helpers doing all the work. Your apple supplier is even polishing, shining and delivering your apples to the stall, which means you have very little to do. Maybe you should cut your salary to the same as Debra's?"

Jo agreed. She understood the logic and she also thought the helpers would understand how important it was to keep all the costs controlled.

Sage quickly changed the numbers and put them on the screen so Squawk could comment.

Pricing for Chockas

Chockas		5,000
Other costs:		
Debra 50%		175
Overheads:		
Jo 50%		175
Ted 50%		75
Sage 50%		75
Total cost		5,500
Profit	20%	1,100
Estimated Sales	200	6,600
Price for 1		33

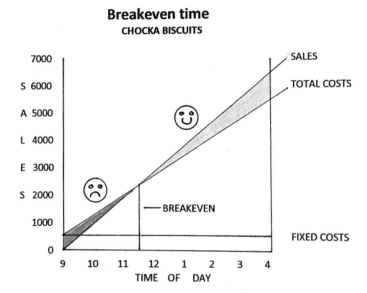

Breakeven time
CHOCKA BISCUITS

Squawk looked at the Chocka numbers carefully. "The pricing looks right, you have reduced risk by controlling the fixed costs, and you only have to sell about 30% of the Chockas to cover your costs, so by 11.30 you are making a profit."

Pricing for Apples

Apples		700
Other costs:		
Debra's friend		150
Debra 50%		175
Fixed costs		
Jo 50%		175
Ted 50%		75
Sage 50%		75
Total cost		1,350
Profit	20%	270
Estimated Sales	100	1,620
Price for 1		16

Then Sage put the apples business numbers on the screen.

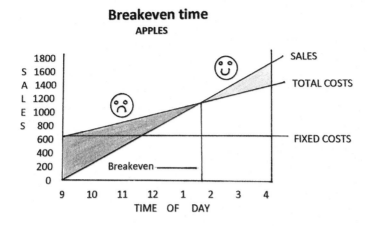

Breakeven time
APPLES

Squawk again looked on intently. "Mmm," he said, "I think you may have reduced your price too much because your fixed costs are high in comparison to sales of 1,620p. You have to sell over 70% of the apples before you cover your fixed costs. If you can, decrease your fixed costs or increase the price to 19p. Remember MAGIC STEP 1?"

MAGIC STEP 1:
Even small changes in the price you charge for your product/services can make a HUGE difference to your profit

"Increasing the price to 19p will double your profit and you will cover your costs before lunchtime."

Jo agreed. After all, this still meant she had reduced the price by 15% compared to the 22p she charged before, and she quickly got Sage to change the calculations.

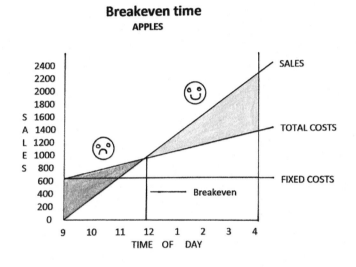

Breakeven time
APPLES

Happy before lunchtime!

So as time moved on there were lots of mice for Jo to train in baking and Mr Ted went and sat in the sun and thought a lot.

Jo put the price of Chocka biscuits up to 34p (she added a little more because she was worried about some Chockas going missing or being broken), which was still competitive according to Mr Ted's research.

When customers asked why the price had gone up, Jo replied, "Yesterday was an introductory offer. You were lucky, and as a special bargain I have put apple prices down! Enjoy your day."

SQUAWK'S ACTION POINTS FOR ALL BUSINESSES:
MAGIC STEP 4: MINIMIZE FIXED COSTS.

- **Continually review all your fixed costs.**
  Confirm they are adding value to your
  customer offering. Be vigilant: businesses
  always change, and no product remains
  dominant forever. An old client of ours
  had a division that was the market leader
  printing chequebooks, which historically
  had strong sales and high margins. Then
  the demand for these reduced dramatically
  but their fixed costs had not. Think of
  other products where sales collapsed: oil,
  video rental stores, telephone directories,
  Blackberry phones, fax machines, cameras
  and travel agents to name a few. When will

it happen to you? Or has it? Check! Keep focused on fixed costs because they do not fall as fast as sales.

- **Do not take on any new fixed costs without challenging them**. They have to be paid every day regardless of how many items you sell. Only take on fixed costs if you have researched all options for a direct cost option. For example, buy computing power from the cloud rather than investing in servers.

- **Outsource activities**. Continually review all business activities and outsource where possible, converting fixed costs into direct ones.

- **Ensure continuity of supplies**. Make sure you have a product to sell all year round because overheads are there 365 days of the year.

- **Always have a proactive Sage**. Real-time reporting means you can rectify mistakes straight away.

SUMMARY

Grandpa invited Jo to have a cup of tea with him to discuss the journey they had travelled.

Jo was happy she was now making a profit of 1,640p a day compared to the 100p in her very first plan. Even more importantly, all of her learning was focused around the **4 MAGIC STEPS** to doubling profit:

MAGIC STEP 1:
Even small changes in the price you charge for your product/services can make a HUGE difference to your profit

MAGIC STEP 2:
Changes in the volume of your sales quickly affect your profit

MAGIC STEP 3:
Control your costs. Not doing so can wipe out profit

MAGIC STEP 4:
Minimise fixed costs because they have to be paid every day regardless of how many items you sell

Jo's journey took her profit from 100p in her first business plan to her current 1,640p – clearly more than double. Along with the 4 MAGIC STEPS, in her journey she learned some important lessons:

- Targets and Plans set the discipline required to achieve a profit.

- The importance of charging the right price.

- How being creative and introducing new lines can lead to selling more of existing products.

- How to reduce costs by focusing on economic activities, making sure resources are used efficiently.

- Being prepared to make painful decisions to keep costs low, including changing suppliers and reducing the wages bill.

- Continually looking to new suppliers to ensure you are sourcing the most efficiently made product.
- Being mean on fixed costs reduces risk: the fewer fixed costs, the earlier in the day you can make a profit.

Jo's journey helped her to more than double the profit of her business. Using the 4 MAGIC STEPS to doubling profit means you can too.

SQUAWK'S CHALLENGE TO BUSINESS LEADERS:

- Do you know the source of your current net profit?

- Do you know the net profit generated by each of your main product lines, or by each of your customers or even by geography?

- Create competition between the senior managers leading each of the 4 Magic Steps.

- Find a 'Grandpa' or 'Squawk' to act as a mentor/confidant who can facilitate the steps required. Being a CEO is a lonely place.

- Show your interest as the leader of the business to demonstrate your commitment to growing profit.

Task your senior managers to:

- Determine the current profit levels for each of your main product lines, customers and/ or geography.

- Set targets for each of the 4 Magic Steps in their areas.

- If it is genuinely not possible to get growth in sales or improvement in price, then transfer that target to one of the other steps.

- Cascade these simple targets throughout the business and monitor monthly.

- Celebrate each achievement along the way and feed the progress back to the whole business.

SQUAWK'S CHALLENGE TO ENTREPRENEURS:

You know the concept, product or service that you want to make into a business, so have the faith and remember SAVE ME – take the first step, make a target and a business plan. Then find a 'Grandpa' or 'Squawk' to act as a mentor and advisor. But most important of all remember the 4 Magic Steps:

MAGIC STEP 1:

Even small changes in the price you charge for your product/services can make a HUGE difference to your profit

MAGIC STEP 2:

Changes in the volume of your sales quickly affect your profit

MAGIC STEP 3:

Control your costs. Not doing so can wipe out profit

MAGIC STEP 4:

Minimise fixed costs because they have to be paid every day regardless of how many items you sell

ACKNOWLEDGEMENTS

Growing up in a family business environment meant that I used to sit on my father's knee talking about 'business'. He would ask, "Why did we do that? What were the effects? Would you do it? What might go wrong? What else should we do?" How grand it was. How can a pre-teen child really enjoy balance sheets? Well, I did. Rumour has it that he used to whisper in my ear every night that I was going to become an accountant. And guess what? I did. I was in awe of him. I just didn't understand how he 'knew' things would work. Until the huge depression of the 1970s he loved business, it was his hobby, his life. He loved helping people but this backfired when a heart attack caught him out. Typical for him, this was related to bankrolling a friend's failing property business. The last time I saw him I was angry with him for the stress he was creating, but he just said "I wanted to help".

In retrospect I guess I did get his innate ability to intuitively understand and enjoy business so this is a belated thanks.

I am of course grateful to all those who have given me encouragement to write this book: my wife Ros was always stubborn in saying, "Just get on with it". She could not understand why I was hesitant – just like my father, she knew I could do it!

Also to Peter – you gave me that confidence.

Thanks to Tim, Sophie and Katie for helping get the book into the public domain, thanks to Ruth for taking the time and energy to write the foreword and also to those who took time to review the book.

However, a special thanks must go to the illustrator Richard Mayes. What a genius!